THE DARK VALLEY

...WHEN YOUR FAITH BECOMES SHAKEN

EGBUCHUNEM ONYEKANNA

Made with ♥ on the Notion Press Platform
www.notionpress.com

In loving memory of my dear sister Amy Obiomo
Okwupkai nee Egbuchunem

Contents

Preface

I experienced the personal loss of my sister. Many who came around at that time just to console the family said things like, 'we shouldn't question God; God gives and takes; He knows best'. To be honest, those words made me hurt even more.

As a young Christian, at that time, that loss made me question so many things; I questioned God's love, his power, and I questioned my faith. It was a dark and hard time for me. Looking back I am glad for the help of the Christian brothers and sisters who prayed for me.

I believe that the truth about the crisis of faith needs to be shamed, because so many Christians are going through it.

Ted Turner, the media mogul, lost his faith after his sister died of a painful disease. Turner claimed, "I was taught that God was love and God was powerful, and I couldn't understand how someone so innocent should be made or allowed to suffer so?

The fact that there are many who once knew the lord Jesus and walked away from that relationship with him as a result of a personal loss, or pain of suffering make it a real and serious issue – one that should be a paramount one for the church.

A personal loss of a loved one, an affliction, a divorce, a job loss can trigger a crisis of faith. The church should be more open to address this issue letting the brethren know that it is not strange to have such struggles. I believe that when people know that they can have these struggles and navigate it without losing their faith they will be encouraged to come out with their struggles.

My intention in writing this book is to be a blessing by helping you navigate your dark valley. Whatever challenges you may be facing or have faced, whatever circumstances are weighing you down, you can come out of it with a deepened faith in the Lord Jesus Christ. I challenge you to read this book with an open heart.

Acknowledgements

Special thanks to everyone who have touched my life with
their own:
Pastor David Eneobong, thank you for laying a strong
foundation of faith in my life.
Elizabeth Egbuchunem, I am blessed to have you.
Reverend Vanessa Hinton, you are a God sent.

I

WHEN TRAGEDY HAPPENS

In my many years of ministering, I have personally encountered many Christians who have at some time had a struggle of faith in their walk with God. This struggle of faith is not talked about in church, and I strongly believe it should be an important one for the church.

I say this because there are many who have left church or renounced faith as a result of this struggle. I also believe there are many others in church who have lost the joy and zeal they once had for serving God.

Majority of Christians folks are so judgmental; when people leave the church or faith they're judged to be canal or immature. Any Christian who is very much defensive about his convictions will always consider those who struggle with their faith as immature. This is the reason those who struggle at some point with their faith are afraid to speak up. They cover it up with a smile, or "I am fine" response, but deep down inside, there is an incredible struggle. The struggle is real and very serious.

In recent times, the Christian community the world over has witnessed prominent worship leaders and pastors renounce their faith, while others committed suicide. I have heard some people respond in shock at a pastor committing suicide. They can't imagine why?

I can tell you this, persevering a struggle of faith is more difficult for those in spiritual leadership.

The pastor's work is to bear the weight of watching over the souls of his congregation. And for this, he's accountable to God (Hebrews 13:17). Pastors are not super humans, they too struggle with depression and anxiety, and the responsibility of watching over the souls of others impact their ability to speak up about their internal challenges. Most pastors are drowning and can't find the strength to share their struggles with anyone.

Surviving the struggles of faith is important because failure to properly navigate it may result in renunciation of faith, deep depression, followed by suicide.

As a Pastor, I can boldly say that I have had times I struggled with my faith. It is possible that you are going through your own personal struggles with your faith, or perhaps, you may know someone who does. The good news is that you are not alone, and it is not out of place or strange that you are having these struggles.

There are a number of great men and women in the Bible who experienced deep personal struggles of faith at one time or another in their walk with God. When we read their stories, there is hope and encouragement knowing that we are not alone and that we can survive this battle.

In Numbers 11:14-15(Amplified), Moses said:

"I am not able to carry all these people alone, because the burden is too heavy for me. And if this is the way you deal with me, kill me, I pray you, at once, and be granting me a favour and let me not see my wretchedness(in the failure of all my efforts)"

Moses came to a point in his life and walk with God, where he felt he could not go on. He experienced a deep personal struggle of faith.

Naomi's struggle of faith is seen in the book of Ruth.

"Don't call me Naomi, she told them. Instead, call me Mara, for the Almighty has made life very bitter for me. I went away full, but the LORD has brought me home empty. Why should you call me Naomi when the Lord has caused me to suffer and the Almighty has sent such tragedy?" (Ruth 1:20-21, NLT)

There are so many people who like Naomi feel that God is responsible for the suffering and hardships in their lives. Naomi experienced a crisis of faith.

Job also experienced a crisis of faith.

"I am disgusted with my life. Let me complain freely. I will speak in the bitterness of my soul. I will say to God, 'don't simply condemn me-tell me the charge you are bringing against me. What do you gain by oppressing me? Why do you reject me, the work of your own hands, while sending joy and prosperity to the wicked?" (Job 10:1-3, NLT)

Job went as far as cursing the day he was born (Job 3:2) because of what happened to him.

Elijah the fiery Prophet of God also experienced a struggle of faith when he fled from Jezabel:

"And when he saw that, he arose, and went for himself, and came to Beersheba, which belongeth to Judah, and left his servant there. But he himself went a day's journey into the wilderness and came and sat down under a juniper tree, and he requested for himself that he might die; and said, it is enough; now, O LORD, take away my life, for I am not better than my fathers" (1 Kings 19:3-4, KJV)

Have you ever felt like you have had enough of what you are going through, that you cannot take it anymore and you just want it to end? Elijah's struggle of faith was just like that.

One thing all of these great bible characters have in common is that they did not lose their faith, even in the midst of deep personal struggles.

Having a crisis of faith is not a bad thing. However, it is the outcome that really matters. If your crisis of faith leads you away from your faith in God, it means you did not handle your crisis well. Properly handling your crisis of faith should move you from that place of spiritual doubt and disappointment towards a deeper faith in God.

Christianity is not all about mountain-top experiences like some preachers would have you believe. On the contrary, the journey of faith consists of mountain-top experiences as well as dark-valleys of doubt. Both of these experiences are significant in our spiritual maturation.

The dark valley is the place of deep personal struggles of faith. It is the place where you feel you have lost your purpose. It is the place where you just want to give up on life. It is also that place where some things do not seem to add up or make sense anymore.

When you find yourself wondering if everything you had believed as a Christian all your life could be wrong, it means you are in your dark valley.

Certain events such as the loss of a loved one, extreme hardship, insecurities, a painful divorce, human suffering and pain caused by acts of nature or terrorism, sickness or disease, can bring us to a pivotal point in our Christian life where we feel we can no longer serve God.

We are so shaken by the things that happen to us that we begin to entertain doubts, and find it hard to connect with the beliefs we have held on to. How can a God who loves me allow me to experience pain, suffering and loss? It just does not make sense.

The death of my sister left me empty and angry. I was a young Christian at that time, and it was a real struggle for me because I couldn't understand why it happened. She loved God and served him, yet God allowed her die in the process of giving birth. It didn't make sense to me; why God allowed her carry that pregnancy to full term only to die in delivery. The painful part was the baby didn't make it. Double tragedy!

I wrestled with my faith at that point, and I just felt that I couldn't serve God anymore. There are no words to describe the anguish and pain of losing a loved one. If you have lost someone you love, I understand your pain, the loneliness and frustration you are feeling.

In our crisis of faith, we may feel distant from God, unable to connect to many things the church stands for, and unable to accept any answers that try to explain away our pains and doubts. In the wake of a deeply personal loss, pain and suffering, faith becomes shaken.

There are moments when we are tempted to think that God just does not care about us, and when we need him the most he is nowhere in sight. It is actually a terrifying moment.

The pain of loss and suffering can be overwhelming and challenging. In our moments of pain and suffering it is so easy to hold God responsible for everything. In Job's moments of pain and suffering he said: "know now that God hath overthrown me, and hath compassed me with his net...he hath fenced up my way that I cannot pass, and he hath stripped me of my glory and taken the crown from my head. He hath destroyed me on every side, and I am gone; and mine hope hath he removed like a tree" (Job 19:6, 8-10, KJV)

Many people's lives are full of suffering and pain, and in those moments some people tend to curse God-venting their frustration and anger by lashing out on God. When Job was afflicted with a terrible case of boils from head to foot, his wife said to him, 'curse God and die'(Job 2:9).

All through history man finds it very convenient to direct his anger and frustrations at God. Is his anger at God justified? Let me make it a bit more personal; is your anger at God justified? I strongly believe that the reason for the anger is the feeling of helplessness-a helplessness to have prevented or even changed a terrible outcome. For example, a little child is diagnosed with leukemia and undergoes an extensive and painful medical treatment only to die in the arms of his parents. The parents are angry at God for allowing such innocent little child go through such pain.

Painful events such as this and others make God appear unfair, weak and cruel thus justifying our anger against him.

I am aware there are some groups of people who use pains, sufferings and disasters as a means to buttress their claims there is no God, or if he does exist, he is not loving and good. These are skeptics whose views of God are narrow and incorrect.

My purpose in writing this book is not to offer some theology into the reasons why there are sufferings and pains in our world. Rather, it is to help you, if you have experienced pain and suffering at a personal level, navigate your dark valley, without losing your faith in God.

I have come across individuals who confessed to me that they lost their faith in God in a time of personal pain and suffering. I have found in my many years of ministering in the lives of people, that there are two major ways people respond to tragedy: they either ask questions or blame God.

Personal loss, pain or suffering can trigger many different and unexpected emotions in people that they respond differently. That is the reason two different individuals can suffer the same tragedy, but respond differently. One may become angry, sullen and bitter with God, that he turns his back on God.

The other, although angry and confused, moves closer to God.

When tragedy occurs, we are faced with a choice: to run to God or become bitter and run from him. When we make the choice to run away from God or turn our backs on him, we forfeit the peace he offers to handle the present hurt, as well as the courage to handle the future he assures. Jesus said; "I have told you these things, so that in me you may have (perfect) peace and confidence. In the world you have tribulations and trials and distress and frustration, but be of good cheer (take courage, be confident, certain, undaunted)! For I have overcome the world. (I have deprived it of the power to harm you and have conquered it for you) "(John 16:33, AMP)

In our moments of deep personal loss, pain and suffering, God offers us his peace. God is not distant or detached from us when we are hurting. On the contrary, he identifies with us in our lowest and darkest moments. The Bible tells me: "since he himself has gone through suffering and temptation, he is able to help us when we are being tempted" (Hebrews 2:18, NLT)

The person referred to in this verse is Jesus Christ, the God incarnate. Jesus entered our world and personally experienced suffering, rejection, sorrows, grief, betrayal and pain. He went through all these so that he'll know how it feels when we hurt. Someone who has not experienced loss, pain or suffering at a personal level will be detached and distant no matter how sincere when he tries to offer comfort to the one suffering.

God does more than sympathize with us in our sufferings; he identifies with us. In fact, he suffers with us. Unfortunately, we are unable to see that because we are overwhelmed with hurt. When our hearts are open to him, we will be able to experience his peace and comfort.

II
ASKING QUESTIONS

In life every one experiences their share of pain, loss and suffering. There is no greater pain and anguish like the loss of a loved one-a mother, father, sister, brother, a child or a friend. The pain of loss can be very overwhelming and challenging. Every pain and suffering has the power to change anyone into a different person; it can make one bitter and resentful or it can make one compassionate and kind.

If you have experienced loss, pain and suffering, you will understand the emotions of shock, anger, disbelief, profound sadness and guilt. All these emotions are vital parts of grief. Another significant part of the grief process is asking questions.

When we experience pain, loss and suffering, the way we often try to make sense out of it is by asking questions: "Lord, where are you?" "Why do you seem far from me?" "What have I done to deserve this?" "God, why can't you just do something?"

Out of our desperation and helplessness we ask such questions. You probably have heard these questions, or you may have asked them at some point.

How could one not ask questions when pained by loss? If you have never asked such questions, it is proof that you have never experienced loss, pain or suffering at a deeply personal level. When we hurt terribly, it is only natural to ask questions.

There are those who believe it is not a good thing to ask God questions when some terrible things happen. If my pain or suffering is intolerable shouldn't I ask questions?

In Matthew 27:46 (KJV) the Bible says:

"And about the ninth hour Jesus cried with a loud voice, saying, E-li, E-li, la-ma sabach-tha-ni? That is to say, my God, my God, why hast thou forsaken me?

Jesus, the God incarnate, in his moment of pain and suffering directed his question at God.

Job, in his moments of great pain and suffering said:

'My complaint today is still a bitter one, and I try hard not to groan aloud. If only I know where to find God, I would go to his throne and talk with him there. I would lay out my case and present my arguments. Then I would listen to his reply and understand what he says to me" (Job 23:2-5, NLT)

If you hurt enough, you will ask questions. The soul desperately searches for answers to at least comfort in those dark moments.

The book of Job in the Bible is a great book. It is a classic text book on pain, loss, and suffering. Job shows us that even when we are deeply hurting, we can still worship God. This man loved and served God, but he lost all his wealth, children, and his health. In a span of 24 hours his world turned upside down.

Someone may be wondering why such tragedy happened to a man who loved and served God? Loving and serving God doesn't insulate us from experiencing some of life's challenges. Bad things do happen to good people!

In his suffering, Job was patient with God; he did not say anything against God. However, things changed when his friends came around him to comfort him. They lectured him about how suffering is a punishment for sin; the greater the sin the greater the suffering. They reckoned that Job must have sinned terribly to deserve his misfortune.

"How long will you go on like this? Your words are blustering wind. Does God twist justice? Does the Almighty twist what is right? Your children obviously sinned against him, so their punishment was well deserved. But if you pray to God and seek the favour of the Almighty, if you are pure and live with complete integrity, he will rise up and restore your happy home" (Job 8: 2-6, NLT)

I consider accusations like this to be stupid and insensitive. I want to state here that not all suffering is our fault. I admit there is a suffering we bring on ourselves as a result of poor lifestyle choices for example; when you are a compulsive alcoholic, your liver gets destroyed and as a result you suffer. The same is true for the drug addict, compulsive gambler and adulterer, who not only suffers but make those related to them suffer.

This is not the kind of suffering I am talking about in this book. Rather, I am talking about those dreadful things we do not deserve that happen to us such as the terror attacks of 9/11, a gun man who opens fire on worshippers in a church, a little child diagnosed with an incurable blood disease, a woman who loses her husband and child in an automobile accident. The accusation or insinuation that such suffering is a deserved punishment for sin is mean.

I believe the fear of being accused unfairly like this hinders church folks from coming out with their secret struggles of faith. It is important we get to understand what someone is going through before we judge them harshly. The truth is that no human being will ever know why terrible things happen to people.

In reading the book of Job I discovered the following:

Firstly, God will never explain to us the reason for our undeserved suffering. It is not because he cannot, but the obvious fact that we cannot understand. This fact is when God replied Job out of the whirlwind:

"Who is this that darkeneth counsel by words without knowledge? Gird up now thy loins like a man for I will demand of thee, and answer thou me. Where wast thou when I laid the foundations of the earth? Declare, if thou hast understanding" (Job 38:2-4, KJV)

God's question as he responds to Job was not to intimidate him. His purpose, I believe is to reveal man's limited understanding of how the world works. If no man knows how the world works, how can he offer explanation to why bad things happen to good people?

God's response was also to humble Job. There is a subtle side of pride that we recklessly and unwittingly yield ourselves to in moments of loss, pain and suffering. It is the one that demands God gives us an answer or we walk away.

That is arrogance! In fact, so many people believe they can do a better job at running things than God. The Bible tells me in 1 Samuel 2:3; "talk no more so very proudly, let not arrogance come from your mouth; for the LORD is a God of knowledge, and by him actions are weighed".

Arrogance has destructive outcomes; to think you know-it-all, when you do not know half of it is arrogance.

Secondly, God was not angry at Job for asking questions. In the same way, God does not draw his punches at us when we ask questions in our moments of loss, pain and suffering.

God understands the depth of our hurt when we lose a loved one; he understands our pain. He takes sides with us when we suffer.

God's anger however was against Job's friends because they did not speak that which was right. The Bible says: "And it was so that after the LORD had spoken these words unto Job, the LORD said to Eliphaz the Temanite, my wrath is kindled against thee, and against thy two friends; for ye have not spoken of me the things that is right, as my servant Job hath" (Job 42:7, KJV)

In trying to comfort someone in times of loss and pain, it is important not to present God as cruel, vindictive or unjust with our words. When I lost my sister, I was in so much pain. A family friend came in the company of her pastor to see my mother. The pastor began to speak saying we should not question God for what happened because he knows best; he gives and he takes. It was those last words he said that made me erupt in anger. I said to him, 'you mean to tell me that God delights in seeing me pain?' The pastor couldn't reply; he never expected such a response especially from a young person.

Is God responsible for human sufferings? Is he a God of sufferings? The amount of suffering in the world raises profound questions about the nature of God, and his involvement in human life. These are points we will do well to remember before offering answers to someone in pain.

When suffering comes, when tragedy strikes, we must never go in the opposite direction of God. We must make the choice to run to him for the answers to the hard questions we seek are found in him. The Psalmist wrote: "send out your light and your truth; let them guide me. Let them lead me to your holy mountain, to the place where you live" (Psalm 43:3, NLT)

By running to God in our pain and suffering, we can discover how he can bring good out of what has happened.

III

MAKING IT THROUGH THE NIGHT

A crisis of faith fuels intensified feelings of hopelessness and doubt. Surviving it therefore, should be a priority.

If the Prophet Elijah could survive his crisis of faith without losing faith in God, it means there is hope for anyone experiencing a struggle of faith though the story behind the crisis may differ.

What wisdom can we glean from the book of Job? How did Job survive his crisis of faith?

The bible gives this account: "when Job's three friends, Eliphaz the Temanite, Bildad the Shuhite and Zophar the Naamathite, heard about allthe troubles that had come upon him, they set out from their homes and met together by agreement to go and sympathize with him from a distance they could hardly recognize him; they began to weep aloud, and they tore their robes and sprinkled dust on their heads. Then they sat on the ground with for seven days and seven nights. No one said a word to him, because they saw how great his suffering was" (Job 2:11-13, NIV)

Surviving a crisis faith will require the unflinching support of friends. You don't have to navigate a faith crisis on your own. Being alone in such a time can be scary and frustrating. It is not the time to push people away or distance yourself from the people who really love and care about you.

I want you to consider two different accounts in scripture that I consider very relevant to the point I am trying to establish.

The first account is in John 5:1-7 (NIV):

"Sometime later, Jesus went up to Jerusalem for a great feast of the Jews. Now there was in Jerusalem near the sheep gate a pool which in Aramaic is called Bethesda and which is surrounded by five covered Colonnades. Here a great number of disabled people used to lie – the blind, the lame, the paralyzed. One who was there had been an invalid for thirty-eight years. When Jesus saw him lying there and learned that he had been in this condition for a long time, he asked him, "Do you want to get well?" Sir, the invalid replied, "I have no one to help me into the pool when the water is stirred"

When we are going through difficult periods, there is this natural tendency to want to be alone. This man in the story suffered for thirty-eight years. In all those years he grew bitter as a result of his condition. My guess is that he was so grouchy that his attitude drove those who came close to him away. There was no one who was there for him. That is an awful state to be in!

This next account is in Luke 5:17-19 (NLT):

"One day as he was teaching, Pharisees and teachers of the law, who had come from every village of Galilee and from Judea and Jerusalem, were sitting there. And the power of the LORD was present for him to heal the sick. Some men came carrying a paralytic on a mat and tried to take him into the house to lay him before Jesus. When they could not find a way to do this because of the crowd, they went up on the roof and lowered him on his mat through the tiles into the middle of the crowd, right in front of JESUS".

This man had the support of his friends in his time of suffering; they were there for him.

Just because you are going through a crisis of faith, doesn't mean you have to isolate yourself from the people who love and care about you. In order to survive your crisis of faith, you must enlist the support of a friend who genuinely loves you. Take the bold step of coming out with your struggles by confiding in that person.

Depression thrives because of our inability to come out with our inner struggles. When you are unable to confide in someone about what you're dealing with, or your inner struggles, it weighs on your soul. It is really a heavy place to be in.

I can tell you this: that many pastors are struggling in silence, because they are ashamed of how people will look at them when they come out with their struggles. They are embarrassed to admit that they have doubts and fears.

Most pastors understand very well the concept of spiritual impartation- and the channel through which grace is transferred from mentor to mentee, or spiritual fathers to sons. However, many find it difficult to admit their deep personal struggles to their mentors – it could be a struggle with infidelity or gambling. When you do not admit your inner struggles to someone, whatever it is you are struggling with will become a stronghold. Sin thrives in secrecy, but when you come out with it, you become accountable.

Having said that, there are certain qualities the person you want to admit you struggles to must possess:

Firstly, this person must be a person of faith. Who better to comfort you and help you in your search for answers than a fellow believer?

"A friend is always loyal, and a brother is born to help in time of need" (Proverbs 17:17, NLT).

Confessing our struggles to a fellow believer allows divine light to shine in, because of their heart felt prayers.

Secondly, the last thing you will need is for your friend to Judge you. Therefore, a vital quality your friend must possess is not being Judgmental. Having a crisis of faith is not the time to start looking for a fault or pointing out one.

"Do not judge others. Welcome those who are weak in faith, but do not argue with them about their personal opinions" (Romans 14:1, GNT).

Thirdly, this person must have the patience to listen. People who are going through struggles of faith are not so much interested in your words of wisdom but in someone who can truly listen to them.

A person may have all the right answers and advice, but if he does not listen, he will not be of help. Every question asked by the one going through a crisis of faith is valid, no matter how absurd it may sound. Therefore, your friend support must be willing to listen and pray for you as well as help you in your search for answers.

Another critical step to surviving a crisis of valley is the willingness to turn to God even with your difficult questions. In the case of Elijah the Prophet, he ran to the mountain of God. When we are going through struggles, the best person to go to is God. If you turn away from God in your moments of crisis, where will you go? The truth is, no one else can help you like God can. The Bible says:

"But (only) with (God) are (perfect) wisdom and insight; he (alone) has (true) counsel and understanding" (Job 12:13, AMP)

"Trust in him at all times, o people; pour out your hearts to him, for God is our refuge" (Psalm 62:8, NIV)

The wisdom and strength of God is available to us in our struggles.

Surviving the dark valley depends on our ability to remember God's faithfulness to us in the past. Most times, pain, loss or suffering can make us forget the times that God had been good to us.

In Joshua 4: 1-7 (KJV), the Bible says:

"And it came to pass, when all the people were clean passed over Jordan, that the LORD spake unto Joshua, saying, Take you twelve men out of the people, out of every tribe a man, And command ye them, saying, Take you hence out of the midst of Jordan, out of the place where the priests' feet stood firm, twelve stones, and ye shall carry them over with you, and leave them in the lodging place, where ye shall lodge this night. Then Joshua called the twelve men, whom he had prepared of the children of Israel, out of every tribe a man: And Joshua said unto them, Pass over before the ark of the LORD your God into the midst of Jordan, and take you up every man of you a stone upon his shoulder, according unto the number of the tribes of the children of Israel: That this may be a sign among you, that when your children ask their fathers in time to come, saying, What mean ye by these stones? Then ye shall answer them that the waters of Jordan were cut off before the ark of the covenant of the LORD; when it passed over Jordan, the waters of Jordan were cut off: and these stones shall be for a memorial unto the children of Israel forever".

God specifically instructed the Israelites to set up a memorial. The question here is why? You see, I believe it is because he knows that man has the propensity to forget his kindness and mercy when going through a difficult time.

When we set up memorials, they serve to remind us of God's faithfulness and kindness to us in the past; how he sent us help when we needed it; how he answered that prayer; how he sent someone to us to give us money or food.

Life may not be fair but, it does not mean that God has not been kind to us.

God's faithfulness, goodness and kindness are some of the things many Christian folks find difficult to understand when going through difficult times. I have come to understand that my difficult seasons cannot stop God from being faithful and kind and good.

God is with me in the very best moments of my life, and he is with me in my moments of pain and suffering. The same is true for you. This is the truth we so often forget when we are going through difficult moments.

When we reflect on how good God has been to us, our faith begins to rise; there is a sense of hope that fills our hearts. It is this hope that enables us to navigate the dark valley knowing that God is with us.

I encourage you to reflect on God's faithfulness to you. God is with you; he has never left you alone. Believe that today and experience the peace he gives.

IV
GOD IS NEVER WITHOUT A PLAN

We will experience tragedies, suffering, loss and pain as long as we are on this earth. It may come as a surprise to most people who believe that God is in control of what goes on in the world to know that he is not. God is not in control!

In the beginning, God gave control of the earth to man. However, when man committed high treason, he (man) ceded the earth to the Devil (Luke 4:6). That act of treason gave the Devil the legal right to rule over the earth. The suffering, pains, sickness, plagues are all acts of the Devil and not God's the whole world lies in the hand of the wicked one (1 John 5:19)

It is important for you to grasp God's nature as revealed in scriptures. God's nature is goodness and there is no evil in him. The Bible says:

"He is the rock, his works are perfect, and all his ways are just. A faithful God who does no wrong, upright and just is he" (Deuteronomy 32:4, NIV)

"This is the message we have heard from him and declare to you: God is light in him there is no darkness at all" (1 John 1:5, NIV)

If you really want to have a clear understanding of God's nature, take a clear look at Jesus Christ, who is the visible expression of the invisible God. Acts 10:38 says:

"Who went around doing good and healing all who were oppressed by the devil, for God was with him".

If Jesus did not go about hurting people, it certainly means that God does not go around hurting people. Every good thing that Jesus did was actually done by his father working through him (John 14:9-10)

God is not responsible for the evil in the world, the devil is. The devil's mission is to steal, kill, and destroy (John 10:10). Tragedy, pain and human sufferings are direct attacks of the devil just to get us to question the love of God and his existence.

So many people are offended by such misery that they question the existence of a good and loving God. They cannot seem to wrap their minds on why a God who loves will allow them to experience pain and suffering?

When we experience personal tragedies, we find it difficult to reconcile God's love and how he could allow such a tragedy. Couldn't he because of his love have used his power to prevent such a tragedy from happening?

The more we ponder this question, the more we tend toward bitterness. When people lose faith in such times of personal tragedy and suffering, they harbor an anger that cuts deep; a resentment and bitterness toward God for not doing anything or something to have stopped or prevented it.

The pain of loss and suffering is very real. When we choose to dwell on the pain of a loss or tragedy, we become stock in the trap of bitterness. Unfortunately, that is what has occurred with many people. Being trapped in the web of bitterness makes it very impossible to see that God is right there with us the whole time.

"The LORD is near to the broken-hearted and saves the crushed in spirit" (Psalm 34:18, KJV)

In order for us to see and understand that we are not alone, and that God is with us even when we suffer, we must honestly weed through the emotions of anger, bitterness and resentment. This will make it easier to accept God's loving comfort.

The Bible refers to God as the father of compassion and the God of all comfort (2 Corinthians 1:3). The LORD comforts us in the midst of our pain as we turn to him in total dependence. He supplies us with strength beyond our understanding.

God can comfort those who turn to him in any circumstance of life. He can quiet every heart. It is just a question of accepting his comfort. Unfortunately, many who are pained by loss refuse to accept his comfort because they are angry. So instead of turning to God, they choose to turn away from him.

God's comfort is major theme in the Bible. The question is why? As long as we are in this world, suffering and pain will be part of our human existence.

I do not know of anyone who has never suffered the death of a loved one, whether father, mother, sister, brother, friend, husband, wife or child. There are people who have suffered the pain of divorce and adultery. There are also those who have witnessed suffering on a much larger scale- wars, famine and disease.

God is compassionate and longs to comfort us even when we are hurting. When we are at our lowest point the

LORD reaches out to us.

Anger, bitterness and resentment will keep us from accessing God's comfort. The Bible instructs us to get rid of all bitterness, rage and anger (Ephesians 4:31).

A vital step towards experiencing God's comfort in the midst of tragedy is personal repentance. That was exactly what Job did:

"You said, 'listen now and I will speak: I will question you, and you shall answer me. My ears had heard of you but now my eyes have seen you. Therefore I despise myself and repent in dust and ashes" (Job 42:4-6, NIV)

We become more open to receive God's comfort when we rid the heart of bitterness. We turn to him in our pain and weakness. In that moment, with tearful eyes, we pour out to him in all honesty our doubts and struggles.

The Bible tells me: "And we know that in all things God works for the good of those who love him, who have been called according to his purpose" (Romans 8:28)

The tragedy may have happened to you but, God has other plans. Most times, it is hard to understand how God can bring good out of a personal loss, or suffering. The truth, however, is that when we trust him, we will see him working through our frustration and pain. There is no experience no matter how painful that God cannot deliver us from. Satan may have brought about that painful experience, but God can turn it for good.

Every painful experience whether it is the loss of a loved one, a divorce or some tragedy, is aimed at extinguishing hope. Hope is a light, and once put out result in depression. But, when we receive God's comfort, he produces Hope. That is the reason it is important that we learn to receive his comfort in the midst of our suffering.

The Holy Spirit pours out the love of God in our hearts (Romans 5:3). It is this love that assures us that we are not alone when we suffer; that his presence is with us. The love of God is comfort in such painful moments. It gives us the peace to handle the present and the courage to step up to the future.

When our hope is fully restored God the uses us to reach out to others. The LORD said to Peter, 'when you yourself have turned again, strengthen and establish your brethren " (Luke 22:32, AMP).

This, I believe was what Paul the Apostle meant when he wrote:

"Who comforts (consoles and encourages) us in every trouble (calamity and affliction), so that we may also be able to comfort (console and encourage) those who are in any kind of trouble or distress, with the comfort (consolation and encouragement) with which we ourselves are comforted (consoled and encouraged) by God" (2 Corinthians 1:4, AMP)

God never wastes an experience no matter how painful. When he has helped you through your pain, you become the right person to help others who are experiencing similar struggles. The deepest hurts can prepare us for the greatest service. The whole essence of Christianity is service to the body.

I may not be able to relate to the pain of divorce no matter how much I tried because I have not experienced it. But, there are people who have experienced it, and now healed as a result of receiving God's comfort. Who better to understand than someone who has been through it? These people are better equipped to help those going through the pain of divorce.

It is important we understand the ultimate purpose of God's comfort. God intends for us to use it in delivering those who are hurting. We must be ready to bless others out of our tragedy. This glorifies God.